Design: Judith Chant and Alison Lee
Recipe Photography: Peter Barry
Jacket and Illustration Artwork: Jane Winton, courtesy of
Bernard Thornton Artists, London
Editor: Josephine Bacon

CHARTWELL BOOKS
a division of Book Sales, Inc.
POST OFFICE BOX 7100
114 Northfield Avenue
Edison, NJ 08818-7100

CLB 4263

THE
LITTLE BOOK
· OF ·

Thai Cooking

*An easy-to-follow guide to creating
authentic Thai dishes.*

CHARTWELL
BOOKS, INC.

Introduction

Thai cooking reflects the influences of both the Indian and Chinese cultures. It has drawn on the best elements of both, that is, the characteristic strong and fiery spices of India, and the speedy methods of Chinese cooking. Added to these two elements are Thailand's own distinctive ingredients including coconut, lemongrass, lime, fish sauce and curry paste. The result of these three inputs is a really exciting cuisine that is not difficult to master. It is a healthy cuisine in which fresh vegetables, served raw or only lightly cooked, play a large part. Oil is generally only added in small quantities, and fish and chicken are more common components of a meal than red meats. In addition, the cooking methods used in Thai cooking such as stir-frying, steaming, roasting, and barbecuing are all simple to use at home. Thai cooking is also quick to prepare and cook, with many dishes taking only minutes to produce from start to finish.

As the attractions of Thai cooking have become well known through new restaurants and media publicity, so the necessary ingredients have become more widely available. Coconut is one of the hallmark tastes of Thai cooking and can be achieved in the West with the use of canned, unsweetened coconut milk. Also available is coconut powder which can be made up with water, and blocks of creamed coconut which can be grated directly into

the recipe or dissolved in water. Lemongrass can be bought fresh in certain Asian supermarkets and foodstores, as can fish sauce and oyster sauce. Other important
ingredients such as green or red chilies, fresh ginger root and fresh coriander (cilantro) are widely available, of course, especially in New York and California.

The most commonly used utensil in Thai cooking is a wok with a lid. Although a frying pan can be used, it is worthwhile investing in this inexpensive piece of equipment.

A Thai meal is usually made up of a selection of savory dishes accompanied by plain boiled rice. The various dishes will include a soup, a couple of meat dishes – maybe a stir-fry and a barbecue, a vegetable dish with sauce, and a noodle dish. The portions of each dish are relatively small, in order that one may taste each one. In Thailand, tiny saucerfuls of delectable savories are sold at street stalls, so that one may pick and choose a variety of tastes to eat together. Thai food should be presented with panache. Each dish should be served with, for example, an adornment of chopped coriander (cilantro) or an exquisitely fashioned green onion flower. The prettiness of Thai food, together with the ease of general preparation and quickness of cooking, makes it the perfect cuisine for entertaining both family and friends.

Curry Parcels

MAKES 18

A tasty snack which can be served any time of the day or as an appetizer.

PREPARATION: 20 mins
COOKING: 30 mins

---

8 ounces chicken breasts
2 tbsps oil
1 small onion, finely chopped
1 cup cooked potato, diced
1 tbsp green curry paste, (see page 28)
2 tsps sugar
18 wonton wrappers
Oil for deep-frying

Sweet-and-Sour Dipping Sauce
1 small cucumber, finely chopped
2 small carrots, peeled and finely chopped
⅔ cup white wine vinegar
2 tbsps sugar
1 tsp chopped fresh coriander (cilantro)

Garnish
Cucumber slices

---

1. Skin the chicken and chop finely. Heat the oil in a wok, and fry the onion and chicken 3 minutes.

2. Stir in the potato, curry paste, and sugar and fry a few minutes. Remove the chicken mixture to a plate.

Step 4 Place wonton wrappers on a kitchen-towel and spoon a little of the filling into the center of each wrapper.

3. Combine all the sauce ingredients in a bowl, and stir until the sugar dissolves.

4. Place the wonton wrappers in front of you on a damp kitchen-towel to prevent them drying out too quickly. Spoon a little of the filling into the center of each wrapper.

5. Dampen the edges with water. Pull up the edges of the dough and pinch together, enclosing the filling. Repeat until you have used up all the filling.

6. Heat the oil in a wok and deep-fry a few at a time 3-4 minutes or until crisp and golden.

7. Drain on kitchen paper. Serve with the sweet-and-sour dipping sauce. Garnish with cucumber slices.

Coconut Shrimp Soup

SERVES 4

Soup is usually served as part of a full Thai meal, but is also served at any time as a snack or meal on its own. Galangal is like mild ginger.

PREPARATION: 20 mins
COOKING: 10 mins

---

1 stem of lemongrass
1 cup raw jumbo shrimp
5 cups fish broth
4 slices galangal
4 Kaffir lime leaves, shredded
2 red or green chilies, chopped
1 tbsp fish sauce
8 ounces whitefish fillets, cut into strips
⅔ cup thick coconut milk

---

1. Remove the tough outer leaves of the lemongrass and discard. Trim ends and thinly slice a piece about 2 inches long.

2. Peel the shrimp, discarding everything except the tails.

Step 3 Pull away the dark vein and discard.

3. Pull away the dark vein and discard.

4. Heat the broth until almost boiling, stir in the galangal, lime leaves, lemongrass, chilies, and fish sauce. Simmer 2 minutes.

5. Add the fish fillets and shrimp and cook gently for 5 minutes.

6. Stir in the coconut milk and continue cooking until very hot, but do not allow to boil.

Spring Rolls with Sweet Chili Sauce

MAKES about 12

Spring rolls are very popular foods to go, but they are are simple to make at home and will taste much better.

PREPARATION: 20 mins
COOKING: 20 mins

---

2 tbsps oil
1 clove garlic, crushed
½ cup ground pork
2 carrots, peeled and cut into thin sticks
2 sticks celery, cut into thin sticks
1 red or green chili, chopped
4 green onions (scallions), sliced
1 tsp grated fresh root ginger
1 tbsp chopped fresh coriander (cilantro)
1 tsp fish sauce
½ cup cooked noodles
About 12 spring roll wrappers
Oil for deep-frying

Sweet Chili Sauce
½ cup canned plums pitted and drained
1 tbsp oil
3 red chilies, chopped
1 clove garlic, crushed
1 tsp sugar
2 tbsps vinegar
Fish sauce to taste

Garnish
Fresh coriander (cilantro) leaves

1. Heat the oil in a wok or skillet and fry the garlic, pork, carrots, celery, and chili for a few minutes, or until the pork is cooked and the vegetables are beginning to soften.

2. Stir in the green onions, ginger, coriander (cilantro), fish sauce, and noodles, and heat through.

3. Place a spring roll wrapper on the work surface and position a small amount of the filling across one corner. Roll up, folding in the corners completely to enclose the filling, as for a burrito. Fill one spring roll at a time, and keep the remaining wrappers covered with a damp kitchen towel, to prevent them from drying out.

4. Just before serving, deep-fry, in batches, for 3-4 minutes until crisp and golden. Drain on kitchen paper and keep warm.

5. Meanwhile, chop the plums very finely. This can be done in a food processor.

6. Heat the oil and fry the chili and garlic 3 minutes. Stir in the remaining ingredients and heat through. Serve with the spring rolls, garnished with fresh coriander (cilantro).

Beef in Oyster Sauce

SERVES 4

You can make this spicy dish very quickly.

PREPARATION: 10 mins
COOKING: 10 mins

---

1 pound sirloin steak
2 tbsps oil
¼ tsp ground cumin
¼ tsp ground coriander (cilantro)
¾ cup baby corn cobs
½ cup canned bamboo shoots, drained
⅔ cup snow peas
2 tbsps oyster sauce
2 tsps soft dark brown sugar
¾ cup beef broth
1 tsp cornstarch
1 tbsp fish sauce

Garnish
Green onion (scallion) slices

---

1. Cut the beef into thin slices and then into strips.

2. Heat the oil in a wok and fry the beef over a high heat for 5 minutes or until cooked. Stir in the spices and cook for 1 minute.

Step 1 Cut the beef into thin slices and then into strips.

Step 2 Heat the oil in a wok, and fry the beef over a high heat 5 minutes, or until cooked.

3. Add the vegetables, then stir in the oyster sauce, sugar, and broth, and bring to the boil.

4. Mix the cornstarch with the fish sauce and stir into the pan, cooking until the sauce thickens. Sprinkle with slices of green onion (scallion) to garnish.

Thai Sweet-and-Sour Fish

SERVES 2

Fish plays a very important part in Thai cuisine, especially in the south. It is often fried in a wok and served with a hot sauce, as in this recipe.

PREPARATION: 15 mins
COOKING: 25 mins

---

1 pound whole fish such as porgy, snapper, or
   bream, cleaned
Oil for shallow-frying
4 green chilies, seeded and sliced
1-inch piece fresh root ginger, peeled and cut
   into thin sticks
2 cloves garlic, crushed
1 carrot, peeled and cut into thin sticks
3 tbsps white wine vinegar
1 tbsp fish sauce
4 tbsps dark soft brown sugar
4 tbsps fish broth
6 green onions (scallions), shredded
1 tsp cornstarch mixed with a little water

---

1. Cut several slashes in each side of the fish. Heat the oil in a wok or skillet and fry the fish about 5-10 minutes each side. Remove from the pan and keep warm while preparing the sauce.

2. Wipe out the skillet and heat a little more oil in it. Fry the chilies, ginger, garlic, and carrot 3-4 minutes.

3. Add the vinegar, fish sauce, sugar, and broth

Step 2 Fry the chilies, ginger, garlic, and carrot 3-4 minutes.

and bring to the boil. Add the green onions (scallions).

4. Stir the cornstarch and water into the wok and cook until sauce thickens. Pour over the fish to serve.

Step 4 Stir the cornstarch and water into the wok and cook until sauce thickens.

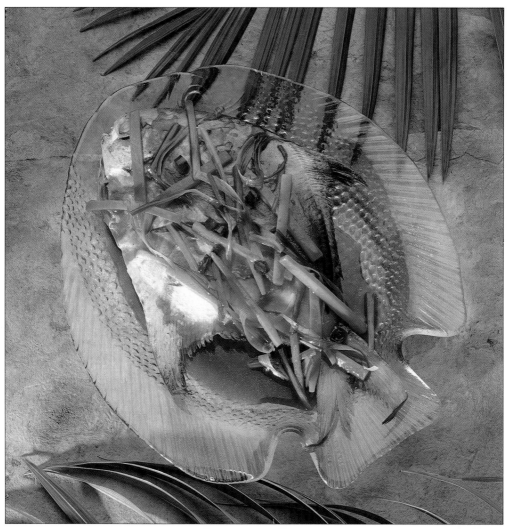

Barbecued Pork

Traditionally, this dish is cooked on charcoal burners by the roadside, but it works just as well in the oven.

PREPARATION: 15 mins, plus 1 hour marinating
COOKING: 20 mins

---

4 cloves garlic, crushed
⅔ cup light soy sauce
2 tbsps soft dark brown sugar
1 tbsp grated fresh root ginger
1 tbsp chopped fresh coriander (cilantro),
    stems and root
4 star anise or 1 tsp ground anise
Red food coloring (optional)
2 pork fillets
2 tbsps oil
2 shallots, chopped
½ cup roasted peanuts, ground
⅔ cup pork or chicken broth
1 tsp cornstarch mixed with a little water

Garnish
Kaffir lime leaves and star anise

---

1. Mix together the garlic, soy, sugar, ginger, coriander, anise, and a few drops of food coloring if wished, to make a marinade.

2. Place the fillets in a shallow dish and add the marinade. Turn the pork over so that it is

Step 3 Test pork with a skewer, the juices should run clear.

fully coated in the marinade. Leave to marinate at least 1 hour, turning once.

3. Remove the meat from the marinade and place on a trivet in a roasting dish. Roast in a preheated oven at 375°F, for 20 minutes, or until pork is cooked. Baste once or twice with the marinade. Test the pork with a skewer, the juices should run clear.

4. Just before the end of the roasting time, heat the oil in a wok and fry the shallots until tender and beginning to brown. Stir in the ground peanuts, the marinade, and broth. Cook until simmering, then add the cornstarch mixture and cook a little longer, until thickened.

5. To serve, slice the pork and pour the sauce over it. Garnish with lime leaves and star anise.

Stir-Fried Chicken with Ginger

SERVES 4

A popular Thai dish served in many restaurants.

PREPARATION: 15 mins
COOKING: 10 mins

---

2 tbsps oil
2 cloves garlic, crushed
2 shallots, chopped
12 ounces skinned and boned chicken breast,
  cut into thin strips
2-inch piece fresh root ginger, peeled and cut
  into shreds
2 Kaffir lime leaves, shredded
2 tbsps whole blanched almonds
½ cup long or French beans, cut into
  2-inch lengths
1 red bell pepper, cut into strips
3 tbsps water chestnuts, sliced
3 tbsps fish sauce
1 tbsp sugar

Step 1 Fry the garlic and shallots until beginning to soften.

Step 3 Add the sauce.

1. Heat the oil in a wok and fry the garlic and shallots until beginning to soften. Add the chicken and fry until it turns color.

2. Add the ginger, lime leaves, almonds, beans, pepper, and water chestnuts. Stir-fry, tossing the ingredients frequently, for 5 minutes, or until vegetables are cooked but still crisp.

3. Stir in the fish sauce and sugar and serve with rice or noodles.

Mussaman Curry

SERVES 4

This curry illustrates the Indian influence on some of Thailand's cuisine.

PREPARATION: 25 mins
COOKING: 1 hour

4 cardamom pods
½ tsp coriander seeds
½ tsp caraway seeds
2 whole cloves
5 small red chilies, chopped
1 clove garlic, crushed
1 stem lemongrass, coarsely chopped
2 green onions (scallions), chopped
¼ tsp grated fresh root ginger
¼ tsp ground nutmeg
1 tbsp oil
1½ pounds sirloin steak
Oil for shallow-frying
3 cups potatoes, peeled and cut into chunks
2-3 onions, peeled and cut into wedges
2 cups thin coconut milk
2 tbsps soft dark brown sugar
1 tsp tamarind juice

Garnish
Chopped fresh coriander (cilantro) leaves

1. Crush the cardamom pods with the side of a knife, and remove the seeds.

2. Place the coriander seeds, caraway seeds, cardamom, and cloves in a wok and dry-fry 1 minute, tossing frequently to prevent burning. Remove from the heat.

3. Mix the fried seeds, chilies, garlic, lemongrass, green onions (scallions), ginger, nutmeg, and oil. Pound together in a mortar with a pestle.

4. Slice the beef into ½×2 inch chunks.

5. Heat the oil for shallow-frying in a wok and fry the potato and onion wedges 5 minutes or until they begin to soften, then remove.

6. Add the meat to the pan and fry until browned. Stir in a quarter of the coconut milk and simmer gently 30 minutes or until meat is very tender.

7. Remove the meat from the pan with a slotted spoon and set aside. Add the chili mixture to the pan and boil rapidly for 5 minutes, then blend in the remaining milk.

8. Return the meat, onions, and potatoes to the wok. Stir in the sugar and tamarind juice. Cook gently for 20 minutes. Garnish with coriander (cilantro).

Five-Spice Pork (See-Krong Moo Ob)

SERVES 4

Serve this delicious, sweet, spicy dish with rice.

PREPARATION: 10 mins
COOKING: 15 mins

1½ pounds pork belly strips
2 tbsps oil
1 tbsp green curry paste (see page 28)
2 tbsps fish sauce
1 tbsp light soy sauce
2 tbsps sugar
1 tsp five-spice powder
1 tbsp chopped lemongrass

Garnish
Fresh coriander (cilantro) and lime twists

---

1. Cut the pork strips into 1½-inch chunks.

2. Heat the oil in a wok and fry the curry paste 2 minutes. Stir in the fish sauce, soy sauce, sugar, five-spice powder, and lemongrass. Cook a further 3 minutes.

3. Add the pork to the wok and cook, tossing it frequently, for 10 minutes until pork is cooked.

Step 2 Fry the curry paste for 2 minutes, stir in the fish sauce, soy sauce, sugar, five spice powder and lemongrass.

Step 3 Add the pork and cook, tossing it frequently.

4. Serve garnished with fresh coriander (cilantro) and lime twists.

Chicken with Chili and Basil

SERVES 4

*Three kinds of basil are used in Thailand. Bai Horapa is the nearest to European basil.
Look out for the other Thai varieties in Oriental food stores.*

PREPARATION: 20 mins
COOKING: 20 mins

4 chicken quarters
3 large red chilies, seeded and chopped
1 tbsp chopped fresh coriander (cilantro) root
   and stem
2 cloves garlic, crushed
3 tbsps oil
2 green chilies, sliced
2 tbsps fish sauce
1 tbsp oyster sauce (optional)
Small bunch basil, torn into small pieces

Garnish
Chili "flowers"

Step 4 Return the chicken to the pan add green chilies, fish sauce, and oyster sauce.

Step 1 Cut the chicken into smaller pieces.

1. Cut the chicken into small pieces, using a large sharp knife or meat cleaver.

2. Pound the red chilies, coriander (cilantro) and garlic together in a mortar with a pestle.

3. Heat the oil in a wok and fry the chicken until golden and almost cooked. Remove from the pan.

4. Add the chili paste and fry for a few minutes. Return the chicken to the pan and add the green chilies, fish sauce, and oyster sauce, if using. Cook over a medium heat 5-10 minutes, or until the chicken is completely cooked.

5. Stir in the basil leaves and serve garnished with chili "flowers".

Shrimps in Green Curry Paste

SERVES 2-3

This is the hottest of Thai curries because of the large number of small green chilies traditionally used.

PREPARATION: 15 mins
COOKING: 10 mins

Green Curry Paste
10 green serrano, pequin or other small chilies, chopped
3 cloves garlic, crushed
2 stems lemongrass, roughly chopped
3 green onions (scallions), chopped
1 tsp grated fresh root ginger
1 tsp coriander (cilantro) seeds
1 tsp caraway seeds
4 whole cloves
1 tsp ground nutmeg
1 tsp shrimp paste
3 tbsps oil

Curry
1 cup thick coconut milk
2 tbsps green curry paste
1½ cups peeled, raw shrimps
1 tbsp fish sauce

Garnish
Lemon rind, thinly peeled

1. Make the curry paste by placing all the ingredients in a food processor and grinding together. Store in a small jar in the refrigerator until required.

Step 2 Heat a little of the coconut milk in a wok and add the curry paste. Boil rapidly 5 minutes.

2. Heat a little of the coconut milk in a wok and add 2 tbsps of the curry paste. Boil rapidly 5 minutes, stirring frequently, then reduce the heat.

3. Gradually stir in the remaining coconut milk, then add the shrimp and fish sauce. Cook gently about 5 minutes or until the shrimp are cooked. Garnish with lemon rind.

Step 3 Gradually stir in the remaining coconut milk, then add the shrimp and fish sauce.

Spicy Steamed Pork with Noodles

SERVES 4

Noodle dishes like this are served as part of the main course or as a snack at any time of the day.

PREPARATION: 20 mins
COOKING: 20 mins

1 cup ground pork
1 tsp ground coriander (cilantro)
1 tsp ground cumin
1 tsp ground turmeric
Beaten egg, (optional)
1 bunch bok choy or spinach, washed
1-2 tbsps green curry paste (see page 28)
1 tsp shrimp paste
⅔ cup thick coconut milk
6 ounces egg noodles

Garnish
Chopped fresh coriander (cilantro)

1. Place the ground pork and spices in a food processor and process until very finely chopped. Shape the pork mixture into small balls, using damp hands. (If you do not have a food processor, mix the ingredients together and add a little egg to help bind the mixture together.)

2. Tear the bok choy into large pieces and place in a heatproof dish that will fit into a steamer. Arrange the pork balls on top.

3. Mix together the curry paste, shrimp paste,

Step 2 Tear the bok choy into large pieces and place in a heat-proof dish that will fit into a steamer.

Step 3 Mix together the curry paste, shrimp paste, and coconut milk, and pour over the pork balls.

and coconut milk, and pour over the pork balls. Cover and steam for 20 minutes.

4. Meanwhile, cook the noodles as directed on the package. Mix the noodles with the pork and bok choy, or arrange noodles on a platter and pile the pork mixture on top. Garnish with a sprinkling of chopped coriander (cilantro) leaves.

Thai Fried Rice

SERVES 4-6

Add different fresh vegetables to the rice according to what you have to hand. Serve as side-dish or as a meal in itself.

PREPARATION: 15 mins
COOKING: 15 mins

A little oil
1 egg, beaten
1 tbsp thin coconut milk
1 cup chicken breasts, skinned and cut into small pieces
1 cup raw, peeled bay shrimp
1 small red or green chili, seeded and chopped
1 tbsp green curry paste (see page 28)
2 tbsps fish sauce
6 cups cooked rice
1 cup green or wax beans, cut into 1-inch lengths
6 green onions (scallions), sliced diagonally

Garnish
Chilli "flowers"

1. Heat a wok and brush with a little oil. Beat the egg and coconut milk and pour into the wok. Swirl the wok so that the egg coats it, to form a thin omelet.

2. Cook a minute until just brown on the bottom, then flip over and cook the other side.

3. Remove from the wok and allow to cool slightly. Roll up and cut into thin strips.

4. Heat a little more oil in the wok and add the chicken and bay shrimp. Cook quickly, stirring frequently.

5. Add the chili, curry paste, and fish sauce to the pan and heat until sizzling hot. Stir in rice, beans, and green onions (scallions).

6. Reduce the heat slightly and cook, stirring constantly, until the rice is hot.

7. Pile onto a serving dish and garnish with shredded egg and chili "flowers".

Step 7 Pile onto a serving dish, and garnish with shredded egg and chili "flowers".

Mixed Vegetable Stir-Fry

SERVES 4

Very fresh vegetables cooked quickly and simply play a large part in Thai cuisine as this dish shows.

PREPARATION: 15 mins
COOKING: 6 mins

Prik Dong
6 red or green chilies
6 tbsps white wine vinegar

2 tbsps oil
3 cloves garlic, crushed
1 shallot, sliced
1 cup each cauliflower and broccoli, divided into small flowerets
1 small red bell pepper, sliced
½ cup snow peas
½ cup baby corn cobs
½ cup green or wax beans, cut into 2-inch lengths
2 carrots, peeled and sliced
⅓ cup fresh or canned straw mushrooms
2 tsps light brown sugar
1 tbsp light soy sauce

---

1. Slice chilies diagonally and combine with the vinegar to serve as a dipping sauce for the vegetables or noodles.

2. Heat the oil in a wok and add all the vegetables together.

3. Stir-fry 4 minutes, or until vegetables are cooked but still crisp.

4. Stir the sugar into the soy sauce and add to the wok. Toss well and serve. Serve with the dipping sauce.

Sautéed Bean Sprouts

SERVES 4

A simple vegetable dish which can be served with a hot dipping sauce if wished or as a foil to a hot curry.

PREPARATION: 5 mins
COOKING: 5 mins

2 tbsps oil
8 green onions (scallions), thickly sliced
3 cups bean sprouts, rinsed and drained
1 cup cooked, peeled shrimp (optional)
½ small head of Chinese (Nappa) cabbage, shredded
1 tbsp fish sauce

1. Heat the oil in a wok until sizzling then add the green onions (scallions), bean sprouts and shrimp, if using. Stir-fry for 1-2 minutes.

2. Add the Chinese (Nappa) cabbage and toss over a high heat for about 1 minute, or until just beginning to wilt.

3. Stir in the fish sauce and serve immediately with a dipping sauce of your choice.

Step 2 Add the Chinese (Nappa) cabbage and toss over a high heat.

Step 3 Stir in the fish sauce and serve immediately.

Coconut and Banana Pancakes

SERVES 4

These coconut pancakes with a tangy lime-and-banana filling are delicious served warm or cold.

PREPARATION: 15 mins, plus 20 mins standing
COOKING: 15 mins

1 cup rice flour
Pinch of salt
2 eggs
1¼ cups thin coconut milk
Green food coloring, (optional)
2 tbsps shredded coconut

Filling
Grated rind of ½ lime
2 tbsps lime juice
1 tsp sugar
1 tbsp shredded coconut
2 bananas

Oil for frying

1. Place the flour and the salt in a mixing bowl and make a well in the center. Drop in the eggs, and a little of the milk.

2. Using a wooden spoon, beat well, slowly incorporating the flour until you have a smooth, thick paste.

3. Gradually beat in the remaining milk. Stir in a few drops of food coloring, if used. Allow to stand 20 minutes.

4. Just before using the mixture, stir in the coconut.

5. Meanwhile, make the filling. Mix together the lime rind, juice, sugar, and coconut. Slice the bananas and toss in the mixture.

6. To cook the pancakes, heat a little oil in an 8-inch heavy-based skillet. Pour off excess oil. Spoon about 4 tbsps of mixture into the pan and swirl to coat the pan. Cook about 1 minute, or until the underside is golden.

7. Flip or toss pancake over and cook the other side. Slide the pancake out of the pan and keep warm. Repeat until all the batter is used. Fill pancakes with bananas and serve immediately.

Thai Fruit Platter with Coconut Sauce

SERVES 4

Usually a simple Thai meal will finish with fresh fruits. If oriental fruits are not available, use South American fruits, such as guava, fejoa, sapote, sweetsop, etc.

PREPARATION: 30 mins

Selection of Thai Fruit such as:
Lychees
Rambutans
Mango
Pineapple
Watermelon
Cantaloupe melon
Papaya
Starfruit (carambola)
Bananas

Coconut Sauce
1½ cups thick coconut milk
2 tbsps superfine sugar

1. Prepare the fruit; peel the lychees or rambutans, starting at the stem end.

2. Cut the mango in half either side of the large central stone, peel, and slice the flesh into fingers.

3. Cut the pineapple into wedges, and peel them if you like.

4. Cut the melons and papaya in half and discard the seeds. Peel and slice.

Step 2 Cut mango in half and slice into fingers.

Step 4 Peel and slice melon and papaya, discarding the seeds.

5. Slice the starfruit (carambola).

6. Cut the banana diagonally into chunks and toss in lemon juice.

7. Arrange the fruit on a serving platter.

8. Make the sauce by combining the coconut milk and sugar. Pour the sauce over the fruit or serve in a bowl or jug.

Sticky Rice with Mango and Star Fruit

SERVES 4

Sweet, glutinous (sticky) rice is served in many forms as a dessert in Thailand. This delicious version is served with mango and starfruit (carambola).

PREPARATION: 10 mins, plus overnight soaking
COOKING: 30 mins, plus 15 mins standing

2 cups glutinous or sticky rice
2 cups thick coconut milk
3 tbsps sugar
Pinch of salt
1 mango
1 starfruit (carambola)

1. Soak the rice overnight in cold water.

2. Line the top of a steamer with cheesecloth. Drain the rice and place in the steamer. Cover and steam for 25 minutes. The rice will be just tender but not fully cooked.

3. Combine the coconut milk, sugar, and salt in a saucepan and heat gently. Stir in the steamed rice and simmer for 2 minutes.

Step 2 Drain the rice and place in the steamer, cover and steam for 25 minutes.

4. Remove from the heat, cover, and leave to stand 15 minutes. The rice will continue to cook in this time.

5. Cut the mango in half as close to the large central stone as possible. Remove the peel, and slice. Slice the starfruit (carambola).

6. Arrange the fruit and rice attractively on serving dishes.

Index